Kashavera's Emotions

Kashavera S. Williams

PublishAmerica
Baltimore

© 2006 by Kashavera S. Williams.
All rights reserved. No part of this book may be reproduced, stored in a retrieval system or transmitted in any form or by any means without the prior written permission of the publishers, except by a reviewer who may quote brief passages in a review to be printed in a newspaper, magazine or journal.

First printing

ISBN: 1-4241-2782-3
PUBLISHED BY PUBLISHAMERICA, LLLP
www.publishamerica.com
Baltimore

Printed in the United States of America

I would love to dedicate this book to a number of people; being that I would probably forget a name or two I won't name you individually. I would love to thank God first for all that He's done for me in all of my life, even when I back slid, he still loved and saved me from a lot of things. I then would love to thank all of my parents. The first two for creating me, and the last two for taking care of me. I would like to dedicate this book especially to my daddy Leo who passed and who we miss. To my brother Aaron, who also passed and who we miss as well. To my friends who support me. To my enemies who helped me to push forward. To my teachers who helped me to bring out this gift. My family: brothers, sisters, and cousins. To my publishing company for giving me the chance to do this and last but not least to my future fans, I hope that you really love what you read and hope that you will continue to support me within these next few years, and if I don't come out with anything else within a decade, that you remember me and keep my work close to you.

Thank You,
Kashavera

I would first like to give you a brief warning; this book has poems that have a few bad words in it as well as poems with adult themes. I wouldn't exactly let children under the age of seventeen or so buy this book. I wouldn't want you, the parent, to be angry with me for your children reading such a thing. I would like to apologize for any inconvenience.

Kashavera

A special message to a special friend

I have a special message to say to a special friend.
Look how we start out as strangers to where our friendship begins.
We've been friends for years but now I want more.
I want all of my fantasies to come to life as well as our future to soar.
I tried to hide it inside, however I can no longer ignore.
We should go further and have our future to explore.
I love your eyes, your sexy lips.
You touching my body with your finger tips.
You know what I want, exactly the way I want it.
You know the right things to say and do, I can't wait to get started.
My thoughts and dreams consist of my fantasies of you.
Besides that, loving you is all I want to do.

A Woman Scorned

You let me down in many ways than one,
You asked me for a child, a beautiful daughter or a handsome son.
However for you I couldn't give you either one,
After that making love to me for you was no longer any fun.
I'm sorry my darling for what I couldn't produce,
I came home early from work to see you with another woman you were trying to seduce.
I lost my self-control as my tongue started to get loose,
I told you out of anger that, that night you had to choose.
You chose the other woman; I had to make you pay,
I felt you made your bed in it you had to lay.
Why did that had to happen why did it have to be that day,
I am now sorry; I had to do you that horrible unforgettable way.
You had to understand how deep my feelings were hurt,
You for the longest treated me like a queen, and now you've treated me like dirt.
You use to be so sweet, now I see her wearing your shirt,
You've never been faithful; you've always been this great big flirt.
Why did you make me hurt you, this didn't have to be,
You've run around on me so much you've given me HIV.

All Alone and Dead

When you first meet him, he gives you a handsome smile.
You think to yourself 'I'll give him a while'.
You both are talking; he says what you want to hear.
You never see it coming because soon your smile will turn into fear.
You love the way he hugs and his sexual kiss.
Of course you hope it'll always be like this.
As time goes on he starts to change.
He says and does things that are quite strange.
You find yourself dumbfounded you don't know what's wrong.
Every time you do something he doesn't like his anger becomes strong.
Finally he hits you, punches you right in the face.
You go right into shock as your heart starts to race.
Tears fell as your hands becomes a shade in front of your eyes.
But you never saw it coming; he's good at telling lies.
You stick around in hopes that he'll change.
You do your best to make him happy, so you have this romantic dinner arranged.
You have a nice evening, you're glad that he's happy.
Then you get into this argument, and think to yourself 'I hope he doesn't slap me'.
You must've said something, because he knocks you to the floor.
While he's yelling and swearing he walks up to you kicks you in the stomach and calls you a whore.
We up and wonder, what kind of future lies ahead.
Don't worry my dear there's nothing for you, you're lying there All Alone and Dead.

As a Child

As a child I wanted to be safe and happy.
As a child I got a man that hated and loved to abuse me.
As a child I needed protection from pain.
As a child I got tears running down my face like rain.
As a child I extended my arms to my mother to embrace.
As a child I got punched in the face.
As a child I cried for something to eat.
As a child all I got was knocked off my feet.
As a child I didn't get protected at all.
As a child my stepfather broke my leg and I had to tell the hospital I was injured from a fall.
As a child I didn't want you close, I wanted you to stay away.
As a child I swore I would have my revenge one day.
As an adult I see it every day, I know I need to let it go.
As an adult today I'm afraid to let my love and affections show.
As an adult the memories of the past makes me very sad.
I know for a fact I can't let these experiences drive me stark raving mad.

Come to Me and Let Me In

Come to me, I'll never let you down.
Even if you're not ready, I'll wait till you come around.
Talk to me, my heart and love is only for you.
I want to give myself to you but show me you'll always be true.
Come to me, my heart pounds your name.
You only have your greatness inside of you that I see to blame.
Touch me and show me how you really feel.
Your loving touch, luscious lips, the way you breathe, the words you say, and the way we play will tell me how you really feel.
Come to me, let me know what's on your mind and in your heart.
The more we know the less we would want to break apart.
Why don't you love me the way I love you?
Why don't you do the things for me like I would do for you?
Open your heart to me, what are you waiting for?
You'll see all of the beautiful things God will have for us in store.

Coming Close to God

Coming close to God, coming into his grace.
To my friends I seem odd because I want to see his face.
To reach out my arms and give him a hug.
To feel his holy arms around me feeling comfy and snug.
To tell my Lord thank you for always loving me.
To tell my lord thank you for continuing to bless me and for seeing things through him I see.
I want to tell the lord thank you for lifting me up and forgiving me of all my sins.
To tell the lord thank you for helping me through my short comings.
Coming close to God, knowing what to do.
Having to pray my prayer so God could make them come true.
He came into my life and showed me the light.
Before he came into my life, there was never any sunshine; it always seemed to be night.
Now that Jesus is here he'll never leave my heart.
I don't know what I'll do if we ever fell apart.
When I see Jesus I know exactly what I'll do.
I'll tell him with my heart, mind, soul, and all you've given me, I sincerely love you…

Dream Man Come to Life

To finally feel complete is the best feeling of them all.
I found this man that's so wonderful, sweet, handsome, and tall.
When I'm around him I never want him to go away.
I want to see him constantly everyday.
The way he kisses me is so nice and sweet.
I swear this man sweeps me off my feet.
He's the love of my life and I know it's so soon.
I feel like I'm on top of the world, like I can touch the stars and the moon.
My heart pounds his name every chance that it gets.
I love him so much I don't have time for regrets.
He's the man in my dreams that came to real life.
I can't wait to bare his children and become his wife.
I love him so much oh my it's true.
When I see him I'll say I'm head over heels, crazy or madly in love
with you.

Feelings Like This

My heart is pounding.
His heart is near.
I find him astounding.
I'm glad he's here.
To share this kiss.
To spread his love.
To touch like this.
I hear the angels above.
Telling me he's the one.
I still can't believe.
This person is loving me, and we're actually having fun.
This is the one I want to achieve.
To let this grow stronger and make this last.
To let this go forward and never look back to the past.

God Forbid Part I

You live your life by God forbid.
Now I understand why your silly self hid.
You're walking down the street at night and the only way home is down a dark alley.
You turn around to go back where you came because that's where a bunch of young people rally.
So you of course went on and hid.
You're afraid of getting robbed, God forbid.
You sit alone in the house you share with your family and you hear a noise at the door.
You cowardly run away, making it up in your mind you don't want to live there anymore.
So of course you go and hide.
God forbid there's a burglar coming inside.
You live your life purely based on God forbid.
Now I understand why your silly self hid.
You're hiding from today.
You're hiding from tomorrow.
You're hiding from the way.
You would share happiness and sorrow.
You're hiding from the sun.
You're hiding from the rain.
You're hiding from the fun.
Of healing from your pain.
You're hiding from living it for God.
You're hiding from a husband or wife.
You're hiding from acting as a couple, silly and odd.
You're hiding from perfection.

You're hiding from mistakes.
You're hiding from directions.
You're hiding from the reals and the fakes.
You're hiding from the chance to make yourself strive.
You're hiding from the chance to really stay alive.
You're hiding from the chance to give all you can give.
Oh, God forbid you'll give yourself the chance to live.

Going Through the Emotions

Going through the emotions whether up or down can still bring lots of pain.
Whether happy thoughts make you happy or sad thoughts drives you insane.
Going through the emotions could drive you to the point where you break.
All of them hit you at once, so you try to stay calm for goodness sake.
Going through the emotions can bring you down to your knees.
To try to escape them you guzzle down a 40 ounce alcoholic beverage and smoke some trees.
Going through the emotions makes you feel feelings you wouldn't ordinary feel.
That's when you open your eyes sweetie, and realize there's a serious problem and it's for real.

Guess Who

Back stabbers, you dirty little fiends.
You're not even sociable, you pathetic human beings.
You stab me in the back today, and you smile in my face tomorrow.
A part of me feels you have to pay, but you would just bring more sorrow.
Back stabbers you're no friend of mine.
You're just so jealous because I'm so eloquent and divine.
You think I have more because I seem to have something new every week.
It's nothing but foolish pride you tend to seek.
Back stabbers, oh you back stabbers.
I tell you what; I'll go to the store and buy you the dagger.
To put in my heart because of who you are.
Don't worry people; you don't have to look far.
To find the back stabbers I'll tell you what to do.
Look in the hallway mirror not once not twice but three times and I want you to guess who.
The back stabber my friend, is You!

Hi Mommie, I Understand

My dearest mother, Delores I do understand.
Why you took the abuse from him and how you did everything on command.
I remember all the things he's done to us and how you just stood and froze.
Do the images of your child hood come to you whenever you close
your eyes to doze?
Abuse to you must be normal I have to say to you mommie, it's not.
Just the thought of any type of abuse makes me boiling hot.
The way grandma done you was completely wrong.
Like me, you wanted to feel beautiful and had to stay strong.
I understand as a child you had to emotionally fight.
I want you to know it's not normal to cry for love that you lack.
Someone you can love and who will love you back.
As a baby I had no choice but to love and trust you from day one.
You loved it so much you've decided to have a handsome son.
As the years went by, you've decided to have ten.
Oh please dear mother I hope this is the end.
Now imagine loving ten children and ten children loving you right back.
Unfortunately for you, to foster care is where we had to pack.
I'll tell you something as a matter of fact.
The hugs you gave were great when we knew how to act.

Hiding Before Saying Goodbye

Here I am all alone in the dark.
I could be going outside with my friends or taking the kids to the park.
I'd rather sit here in this dark and gloomy place.
I don't want to hear any laughter or look into anyone's stupid smiling face.
I feel so comfortable here I don't want to leave this place.
This is the only place where I feel I can't go wrong and very safe.
All I need here is music, some food, something to drink, my bed and some air.
I don't want any company I don't want to see you because I know you don't care.
I don't want to be seen by you, in know in here you wouldn't dare touch.
I know when I come out; you wouldn't have missed me very much.
I really don't like it here; however it's not going to hurt.
I don't think I'm going to be here long; you're going to be singing "Precious lord take my hand" while burying me in the dirt.

How Dare You Thank Me Like This?

The anger I feel inside, I need to find a way to let it out,
I could stomp my feet, yell, cry, or even shout.
You hurt me in such a way I truly believe you really don't care,
However, this is the only non-violent way to make you very aware.
I stood by your side when everyone gave you their ass to kiss,
I have one question for you, how dare you thank me like this?

I loved you more than I believed I had inside,
You said you loved me, well, I see you lied.
I would've done anything in this world for you,
You said you'd do the same for me, well, I see that's not true.
You came to me with your problems in tears,
Then, I thought I could trust you with everything, even my fears.
There was one night I needed you, the pain in me was hard to bare,
Guess what, you weren't even there.
You had more important things to do,
I would've never done such a cold thing to you.
I stood by your side when everyone gave you their ass to kiss,
I have one question for you, how dare you thank me like this?

I have to let you go; I have to find new ways,
I know it'll be a while, but I'll have better days.
It'll have to be one way, get you out of my heart,
I wish I could've stopped it from the start.
Now I see the painful truth you used me because of the way I feel,
All the love you said you had for me wasn't even real.
I hope you realize what you've done to me was wrong,
I hope the sadness that'll come from it will be very strong.

I stood by your side when everyone gave you their ass to kiss,
I have one question for you, how dare you thank me like this?

I'm starting to feel better more because you know my pain,
I loved you so much; I saw sunshine in the rain.
It still hurts so much I'm not gonna lie,
Deep down inside I really wanna cry.
You helped me realize that I better not get down I'll have no one to turn to,
That I'm all alone and staying strong is the best thing to do.
I hope that you realize the things I'll do for you is what you do for me first,
To lending me a shoulder to cry on, to a violent out burst.
From now on I'm going to stop thinking with my heart,
We'll either get closer or drift further apart.
Anything good that'll happen between us would be because of you,
If there's anything sweet to happen between us it's because of the things that you do.
I know you would think these actions are quite strange,
I realize towards you I need to change.
So, did you remember how I stood by your side when everyone else gave you their ass to kiss?
Answer me this,
How Dare You Even Treat Me Like shit?

Hush and Listen

Open your eyes and close your mouth.
I don't want you to say a word; I don't want you to shout.
I want you to listen to what I have to say.
Then maybe we'll be a better couple one day.
You say you want to get to know me better but all that mean is getting me into bed.
You said you want me to talk and yet you haven't heard a word I said.
Why don't you stop using tricks to get into my head?
Don't you think I already know and making a fool out of you instead.
You said you want to go out and have a good time.
When in actuality all you are is in your sexual prime.
Don't you understand there's more to me than that?
Don't you want to know me in a manner of fact?
Or do you want to get off and leave me for another?
So you'll get what you get underneath another's cover.
Men, let me tell you something, all women aren't bad.
Some of us, when with you are made quite glad.
I'm sorry for the bad ones from the past.
However when you get with me, just now, it's built to last.
I don't want to go to slow or to fast.
I want you to hold on; you'll see the bad times will pass.
So I'll give you one last chance.
At true love and romance.
If you want me then you may stay.
If not, then good luck finding your love one, one day.

I Can Really Say No to You

Hello you from 'I hate you so much'.
You call to tell me how much you miss my loving touch.
However, I come to tell you that you're too late.
When we got together now I see it was a big mistake.
You weren't the one.
You already have a daughter and a son.
Yet, you tried to make another one.
Not because of love but out of twisted fun.
You wanted a mixed child just to say you have a mixed kid.
Don't you realize how abusive you are to your other kids when you get mad?
When I got the news I wasn't pregnant I was very glad.
Then I knew I can really let you go.
It made me glad to be able to tell you no.
No to my heart.
Which you can never tear apart.
No to my love.
It belongs to my heavenly father from above.
No to my feet.
Because in my heart you've lost your seat.
No to my everything.
Simply because I threw out your engagement ring.
It really feels good now that you've gone away.
Now God can really send that man he wants me to have some day.

I Hate You So Much

I hate you so much, you stupid ass bitch.
You toyed with my emotions; you used me from inch to inch.
You made me believe this 'love' for me was actually true.
All you were doing was paying her back for cheating on you.
I hate your fucking guts they say I'm going to hell.
With the life I've lived with you, boy doesn't that sound swell?
It's like music to my ears except for the fact you'll be there too.
I can't believe how I fell in love and now how you've forced me to hate you.
There are so many things that I truly hate you for.
From the night you conned your way to my heart, to being drunk and you taking my virginity by threaten to sleep with some crackhead whore.
I hate you for all this shit you've put me through.
I stood by your side because my love for you was sincerely true.
You taught me two very special words.

NEVER AGAIN…

Never again shall I fall in love.
Never again will I believe in any from above.
Never again will I let another man in.
Never will I be able to love you again.
Never again will I want to hold another living sole.
Never again will I date a man that's so damn old.

I know that we're only ten years apart.
I'm shocked as hell a man your age doesn't know his own damned heart.

I hate you so much.
I don't want you to look, kiss, hug or to even touch.
I'm glad I'm not pregnant by you; I want you completely out of my life.
I threw your engagement ring away, I don't want a sorry-ass alcoholic like you and I won't honor you by you making me your wife.
That night when you cheated on me, I fought myself not to stab you to death and watch you die on the floor.
I hope you caught some fatal disease you stupid fucking whore.
I hate you so much you stay the fuck away from me.
I hate you so much, I hope someone cuts your dick off and throw it high in the highest tree.

I Know I Love You

I love you so much; I can't get you out of my mind.
I think you're so cute and special, I can't believe they say a good man is so hard to find.
I can't help that you have a special place in my heart.
I love holding you in my arms I never want us to break apart.
You're constantly on my mind even when you're here with me.
When you lean in close to kiss me I find it hard to breathe.
Then that's when it happen, the feelings grew so strong.
That's when I realize there's no way this time my choice could be so wrong.
As we're making out I feel we're the only two people in the world.
The passion between us is so deep, my toes begin to curl.
I just love to look at you and stare deep in your eyes.
I love your romantic gestures and your sweet and special surprise.
I love you so much I hope that's what you see.
My love for you has brought out nothing but the best in me.
I love you so much because you've been faithful and true.
As the years go by, I know I'll fall madly in love with you.

I Love You My Brotha

You've entered into my life at a painful realization of myself,
I vowed because of my life I never wanted a man of color; I would rather have someone else.
When I saw a man of color, all I would see are the men I grew up around,
Sexual abusers, drug addicts, and the ones that beat women to the ground.
I don't ever remember a man hugging or loving me,
None that were real father figures, who kept quiet, plus the abuse, I thought that's the way they all turned out to be.
You led me to believe I was being unfair,
You showed me love talked to me and showed me you sincerely care.
You showed me love and this coming from a man of color is strange to me,
Although deep inside it's scary I feel that if I return the love that's the way it's supposed to be.
I love you as a brother I know it's safe to feel this way,
In you GOD has shone a bright light today.
I love you because you erased most of my fears,
I love you because your smile wipes a way my tears.
I love you because I believe you're my guardian angel GOD has sent today,
Unlike most I believe you're here to stay.
I love you deep down my heart inside,
I love you because you filled me up with joy and new found since of pride.
I love you because you changed my life the way you did,
I love you because you put most of my hatred under a huge lid.
I love you so much my brotha it's true,
I hope to find a man of color just like you!

I Miss You So Much

I need you here I miss you so much.
I miss your wet kisses and your loving touch.
I know when we're together I don't want us a part.
Congratulations you're the one who's embraced my heart.
I love you so much, I need you here with me.
We belong together and should start our new family.
I need you here, I miss you so much.
Since I don't have you here with me, I only have the tears from my eyes to touch.

I Want a Solider

Can you feel the way I feel?
Do you believe you can keep it real?
You girls want a solider, do you know what that mean?
He has to be good and always come clean.
He has to have power and never be a scrub.
He has to come around sometimes even if it means giving you a rub.
You said you want a solider, shouldn't he work for God?
Oops, you look surprised, did I say something odd?
Girl if you say yes I really feel for you.
You'll get a solider all right, and whip your tail is what he's going to do.
Girl, I want a solider to make me feel good.
Do what he must, and all that he should.
I want one to make me smile to see me smile.
One that's going to stick around more than awhile.
'Till that day comes to go to the pearly gate.
So we may speak to God and discover our fate.
To stand strong in his army to fight against the evil one.
To beat him and return to heaven to have some heavenly fun.
I want a solider, one that's in the Army of God.
Oops, once again, did I say something so odd?

I Want to, but You Won't

It's amazing that when I see you I want to hold you,
It's amazing that when I see you smile my heart pounds the way that it do.
It's amazing that when I hear your voice there's one thing that I
really want to do,
It's amazing that when I see you sad, it makes me blue.
I believe that I may know why,
I love you so much it makes me wanna cry.
I want to hold you, but I can't,
I want to kiss you but you won't,
I want to make love to you but you don't.
What can I say?
To make you come my way.
I thought to be patience and wait,
The way we met and fell, I believe was fate.
Come to me and kiss me and make love to me the way I know you can,
Come to me and become my number one heart, my main man.
I love you so much,
From your eyes, to your friendly touch.
Lets go further, what the hell,
Will we last? Only time will tell.

If You Don't Like Me, I Don't Give a Damn!

I have a mind of my own thusly you can't make me feel shit,
I have a mind of my own thusly I think what I want when I want,
however I want people can't stand it.

I have this great smile, I was told more than once that it lights up a room,
Don't you just wish you could sweep it a way with your sad and
depression broom?

When I'm happy I try to make you laugh and be happy with me,
When I'm sad, I try to move a way from you because my sadness
goes from tears to being angry.

When I love you, I love you and when I hate you, I basically just
dislike you,
Well it's just me, what the hell do you want me to do.

The point of this is to basically tell you the way I am,
If you don't like me, personally I don't give a damn.

When I'm not in the mood to smile, it doesn't necessarily mean I'm
angry; I'm just in a relaxed state of mind,
When I'm not in the mood to smile at work, customers take it
childish and say I'm not being kind.

Besides my having an attitude and being a bitch, I can be a loving
person that I'm afraid to share,
That's when people take advantage and I see they don't really care.

I also know how to be a friend, I'm there for you no matter what,
and there's nothing I wouldn't do,
That's one way of knowing if my friendship towards you is really true.

When I fall in love, in you I've found a great person inside,
When I claim you as my man, I do it with happiness and pride.

The point of this is to basically tell you the way I am,
If you don't like me, personally I don't give a damn.

When I'm in love with you, my heart truly pounds, it truly race,
When I close my eyes, the first thing I see is the sight of my true love's face.

Sometimes I hate myself in love because I'm so damn nice,
Towards the end I'm hurting so I'd wish I took my cheating friend's advice.

Nowadays I'd prefer to be angry than to cry because of my pride,
I was taught I had to be strong in order to survive.

The point of this is to basically tell you the way I am,
If you don't like me, I don't give a damn.

My feistiness has gotten me in trouble all of my rebellious life,
With it I lost most of my boyfriends, I doubt I'll ever become a wife.

My feelings get hurt so I may say things I really don't mean to say,
However in a way I want you to hurt the exact same way.

I wish I could be my sweet caring self all the time but I'm scared and don't know where it all came from,
I come from alcohol and drug addict parents who beat me like a drum.

I wish I could be my sweet loving self, but I'm scared to show it in every way,
I need my knight in shiny armor, it's me, and I'll rescue me one day.

Well I'm going to have to quit now, you're learning too much about me,
Sorry till you take the time out to learn me personally, it's the way it has to be.

The point of this is to tell you the way I am,
I know it's not enough; but personally, I don't give a damn…

I'll Finally Admit

I'm here in one area thinking about you.
Holding you in my arms and call you my boo.
Looking admirably in your eyes.
Believing your kiss comes from the skies.
My heart pounds, my soul sings.
Having you close, hearing the bells rings.
What can I do, I don't want to let you go.
Our relationship will last at the top but we must start below.
To build our foundation and truly touch our heart.
To maybe letting each other go and realizing how miserable we are apart.
When I close my eyes I see your face.
My palms get sweaty and heart starts to race.
I'm anxious to see you and tell you how I feel.
We'll last through our trials and tribulations; I know my feelings are real.
God has brought us together.
So in his eyes we'll last forever.
Now I know exactly what I'll do.
I'll finally admit, I'm seriously in love with you.

I'm Tired

I'm starting to see a better picture of my life and I realize it's not the way I want to be.
Nothing but pain, sorrow and lots of blastfimy.
When I was born, I was kidnapped by a woman who wanted me.
Later I was brought back to a man and a woman who had me in foster care by the age of three.
Everyday I would sit and cry.
Everyday I would wish to die.
Now I'm tired of it all.
Feeling all alone with no one else to call.
Not even to say hello.
Neither to my parents or to a loving fellow.
I'm tired of all the fears.
I'm tired of all the late night tears.
I'm tired of all the drama.
If not from some man, but from my own damn momma.
I'm tired of feeling alone.
I'm tired of fighting my heart from turning to stone.
I'm tired of failing at everything I try.
I'm tired of people saying everything I say is a lie.
I hate the way my life turned out to be.
Is this what God had intended for me?
I'll tell you one thing that's definitely true.
To all the people that's hurting me:I'm fucking sick of all of you.

It Doesn't Work for Me

As I open my eyes I no longer see the sun.
I open my eyes wider I no longer see anyone.
Where's all the laughter, I only see the pain?
Where's all the fun? This boredom is driving me insane.
The depression and pain is rising the happiness is gone.
I don't feel very happy and after every failed anything, I'm sick of this same damn song.
No one understands me so I don't say a word.
Every time I find a man, he kills my spirit like a hunter kills a bird.
Where do I go from here what's going to happen to me?
Am I going to be happy as a horse or am I going to sit and remember how these people treated me.
I'm sick of trying.
I'm sick of crying.
I'm sick of failing.
I'm sick of people aggravating me to the point where on them I start wailing.
I don't know what to say about my cloudy day.
Do I do something to pick myself up or do I let it continue to be this way?
I hate to be alone but some people I can't take.
Every time I turn around there's someone being fake.
There's one thing I can't understand.
How do these people get what they want on command?
Is it because I'm not pretty?
If that's it then for them I have pity.
Beauty is only skin deep, it doesn't last forever.
Someone needs to tell them early so they could get themselves together.
Is it because they're skinny and have nice hair?

Oh please! Let me get out and get some air.
I don't know what it is I'm doing so wrong.
People can do me dirty and I can't strike back, but I have to stay strong.
I have to do what I can to get this anger out of me.
Sooner or later I'm going to explode and counting to three won't work for me.

Just a Few Ingredients

I like you wild, I like you rough.
I like you sweet, I like you tough.
I like you honest even with a little white lie.
I like you talking to me and giving me the sexy eye.
I like it when you ease in close as your breath moistens my face.
I like it when you rub your finger tips all over my body as my heart starts to race.
I like the lustful look that comes across your eyes.
I like the way you set the mood so that my body doesn't mind the entering surprise.
I like the rhythm that you have in the bed although you don't have it on the dance floor.
You made it with much excitement, you left me wanting more.
You left me with so much passion and craving desire.
I never thought I'd ever feel this way because my body felt as if it was on fire.
You left me always wondering what's going to happen next.
With all of this passion, desire, excitement, and fire these are just a few ingredients in us having undeniable great sex.

Keeping the Attention off of You

Feelings of anger.
Feelings of hate.
Feelings of danger.
Coming around too late.
You talk about me because I try to do right.
You talk about me because you want me to fight.
You envy me because I even try to go right.
Simply because God took pity on me and showed me the light.
This walk is long.
Trying to do right is hard.
We sing this long song.
To try to play the right card.
Now I'm getting sick of you.
Doing all of the things you do.
There's one thing I'd like to say.
I want you to go away.
I know why you do what you do.
It's because you want to cover up your faults by putting it all on me
keeping the attention off of you.

Look at Our Love

Look at our love, it's so special it's so true,
I've often wondered what's in store for a romance between me and you.
I'm sincerely happy with our togetherness and our passion in store,
The more I think of you, I love you more and more.
My feelings for you I can't deny,
You're the love of my life; the apple of my eye.
Is there anything else I could possibly say?
I'll see what's going to happen when I see you today.

Look at What I Do

He taught me how to love; he taught me how to write.
He came from up above, he brought me into the light.
He saved me from temptations; he loved me from the start.
He delivered me from the evil and all he asks is for me to let him into my heart.
He sent his son down to die on the cross.
All I do is play God and act as if I'm his boss.
He loved me from the beginning, that's why he did what he did.
I pay him back by denying him just the way Judas did.
He gave me this beautiful air.
Every day I act as if I really don't care.
God has saved me through a lot of things in life that I've gone through.
Let me tell you what I do:

As soon as things go bad.
I turn on him and that makes him sad.
As soon as I realize all of the things I lack.
There I go and turn my back.
As soon as I start to feel a huge amount of pain in my heart.
I close the door in his face and quickly break our relationship apart.
When I get angry and cuss my brother to cause him pain.
I drag God's name and use it in vain.
Now that I think about it, I feel as if I crucify him from day to day.
How dare I treat my heavenly father this way?
He doesn't deserve me giving him pain like that.
However on me he doesn't turn his back.
I ask him for forgiveness, I ask him for his love.

I can feel his presence in my heart as well as up above.
I know his love and I'm sure he's aware.
I know that I love him and I will close by saying 'The Lord's Prayer'.

Love from Above

Sometimes I often wonder where my faith in God truly lies.
When things go wrong for me I feel as if he ignores my cries.
The funny thing for me is no matter how I turn away.
He seems to be here everyday.
Reaching out his arms, extending his love.
It's amazing how all his love came for me from up above.

My Angel

You bring lightness to my world as I thought I was in eternal darkness, you've proven me wrong.
It's because of you I can lift my head high, smile and stay strong.

You helped me to see the goodness that I have in me.
You helped me get away from my sad times and made me as happy as can be.

The way we met was strange to the both of us.
Imagine meeting your guardian angel on the bus.

Your voice, your smile, and your words is like an breath of fresh air.
I thank God that you and my best friend were there.

You make me feel safe, you make me feel fine.
I thank God you're a new friend of mine.

I don't know if I could ever repay you for the things that you've done.
However, you make me feel as if I may lose the battle but the war by me will be won.

There's only one thing that I know I can do.
Tell you as a friend and brother in Christ that I love you.

My Enemy

You liar, deceit,
You backstabber, you cheat.
You gossip you freak.
You bastard, my pain is what you seek.
Yes I'm talking to you.
You have a problem? What are you going to do?
You made me this way.
Now you have to pay.
I'm going to take my foot and shove it up your ass.
For what you're doing now and for what you've done in the past.
I can't stand you.
I almost hate you.
I want you to see.
All of the anger you've built in me.
I tell you one thing, if you get up in my face again.
It'll be time for our physical war to begin.

My Idea of the "Perfect Dad"

He's loving and caring even when he gets stern.
He always a part of your life teaching you lessons that you need to learn.
Taking time away from his job and participating with you in sports.
You both wearing matching clothes all the way down to your under shorts.
Taking you fishing, hunting, and teaching you about being a man.
Benching, belching and always lending a helping hand.
If you're a girl growing into a lady.
He'll protect you and make sure you're not too young for a baby.
If the mom and dad break up, he remains together with you.
That's especially what a dad is supposed to do.
His love is unconditional even when he gets mad.
He wouldn't do anything sinister to hurt you because he knows that's bad.
He keeps you and himself in church because with out God he knows what he couldn't have had.
Now that's my idea of the perfect dad.

Dedicated to all of the 'perfect dads' in the world!

My Mother Phyllis Williams

I'm grateful for my mother and all the things she do.
She took in troubled teens like me and you.
Although she was a foster mother she didn't do it for the pay.
She did it so we may turn out to be great men and women like her one day.
As a adult I will admit I'm responsible for some of her grey.
She could have been like the others and gave me away.
She took the chance on me to raise me right.
She punished me just like the others when I came home late one night.
She went to the store and bought me the most expensive shoes I've ever had on my feet.
She went to the store and bought me the best named foods in the place to eat.
There's a lot she's done for me that I'll never forget.
Evening moving to West Virginia is something I'll never regret.
My mother is the type of woman who would take anybody in.
She also taught me that true love starts from within.
We laugh, joke, and have lots of fun.
I love my mother, she loves me, and she loves everyone.

My Very Special Friend

Seeing you makes me happy on a cloudy day.
I wish that I can see you often so I can always feel that way.
You have this gorgeous face.
Your smile makes my heart race.
To hear your voice is like music to my ears.
You make me forget my problems and my fears.
I thank God that I got the chance to be your friend.
I hope to God not to mess it up so our relationship never come to an end.
You're so special to me; we've connected from the start.
That's why you'll always have a special place in my heart.
You make me happy, you make me smile, and you make me laugh.
That's why I've written this poem on your behalf.
You're the greatest person I've ever known.
Within these last few weeks I've wondered if my appreciation for you has ever shown.
Thank you for being there for me and listening to everything I have to say.
I've grown to truly love you each and everyday.
I hope to God that our relationship would never break apart.
If it does, it would completely break my heart.

My Worst Date Ever

We're a couple just getting together.
At least one of us is hoping this relationship lasts forever.
You asked me out and I agreed to go.
You have a motive for asking me, unfortunately I didn't know.
We go out and we laugh and talk.
We then go on the beach for a romantic walk.
Then we get into your car for home, at least that's what I think.
When you stop somewhere unknown my heart starts to sink.
I don't know what's going to happen so I try to keep cool.
Then suddenly you change to this man differently from the man I met in school.
You started to kiss me then your hands got out of control.
You smile in my face as if you're on a roll.
Then, next thing I know, your body got hot.
I wished you would stop, I wished you were shot.
I tried to fight you off but you wouldn't let go.
Then you told me you'd kill me if anyone else was to know.
I felt so embarrassed I felt so ashamed.
I know if I took you to court somehow I would be blamed.
Now I sit and resist every guy.
When they talk to me I act as if I'm shy.
When I reality I want to scream and shout.
Go and find that guy so I can knock him out.
So I can really date and see what it is all about.
Are there any good men out there? We'll truly I'm in doubt.

One-Way Ticket

He purchased a one-way ticket from me; destination my heart.
I knew if I sold it to him, he'll arrive on time take his place and wouldn't break us apart.
I had to finally sell this ticket and it had to be just to the right man.
He had to be very faithful and loyal to his trip because there's no turning back.
Once the plane leaves it's on time and never gets off track.
This man is perfect, he's wonderful already and he has his big bag to pack.
Remember once this ticket is sold, there's no refund, you can't take it back.

Our Children

We see our children play.
We listen to words our children say.
We laughed because we remember being that way.
Do you remember when you use to run?
You didn't care how silly you looked all you knew was that you were having fun.
We see our children sick and well.
We teach our children about heaven and hell.
We see our children doing things we remember.
We see our children as children forever.

Remember Positive

Life for me hasn't been a crystal stare.
At my young age times will get even rougher, so I'm aware.
Sometimes I feel like falling apart and making people feel the pain they make me feel.
I can't do a thing like that and get away with it God is just too real.
Before I break down I think about my past.
Then I realized how long I'd last.
I came from no where, nothing that was great.
I started to feel as if when good things happened for me it's luck and when bad things happened it's fate.
God brought me on Earth for a reason.
I started to believe it was to be everyone's punching bag every season.
I hate my life from start to now.
I know I must make a positive change, I think I might know how.
Have a good heart and love anyway.
Of course, that's going to be hard to remember every day.
Keep up with my faith and always say grace.
I'll have to see God and explain my actions to him one day face to face.
Keep your head up no matter what, life isn't that bad.
Keep a smile on your face, no matter how sad.
Remember it's okay to cry.
Remember not to tell a lie.
Remember to keep going forward no matter how rough the road looks a head.
Remember to stay positive and fun even if everyone else is 'dead'.
If you feel that no one cares for you and don't know what to do.
Remember God truly loves and would know what to do for you.

The Hurricane Is Here

The hurricane is coming,
The fears are starting to rise,
The winds start humming.
The sight of the twisting wind is quite a surprise.
You start to walk fast until you run,
It seems like a race to everyone.
You know you need to get away,
You feel the twister near,
You hope to see another day.
So you can't get frozen with fear.
Now that you're safely afar,
You lose all of belongings including your car.
You lose everything except for the tattered clothes on your back,
The hurricane was so fast you didn't have time to pack.
There was only one thing at the time you really had to know,
The hurricane is coming, you really had to go.
When things are calmed you go back to see your place,
Everything is ruined; your heart starts to race.
You look back again and remember how you saw a relative die,
All you could do is fall down and cry.
I'll tell you something to do today,
Get down on your knees and start to pray.
Remember to hold on, help is on the way,
All you're seeing is night, but remember for you there will be day.
The hurricane came back to the destruction it must finish,
The rubbish that was left it completely diminished.
God will save you, you must believe,
Through him is the ONLY way you can achieve.

Self satisfaction and the completion of building yourself up again,
As soon as you prayed God's plan has already began.
As you pray, we will pray to,
Things will work out for all, especially for you.

The Strength of Children

There are so many children with cancer and fighting for their life.
They don't seem to be built with anxiety; it seems to give them some sort of strife.
Look at them as they laugh and play.
They're not worried about dying; they're waiting to see what's in store from day to day.
Enjoying their mother's love and getting everything that they want.
They're getting spoiled by their older siblings, uncles and favorite aunt.
They know they don't have to worry because God has their back.
Now to you healthy people out there, who want to die, seeing these children's spirits has got to make you feel like a quack?

There Isn't Anybody Else

I have a boyfriend, yet I feel so alone.
My heart feels as heavy as stone.
He doesn't even call anymore; he says he doesn't have the time.
I feel as if spending time with me it's like some sort of crime.
He said that he loves me, but it doesn't sound the same.
He says that he wants me and no one else, but his actions make me feel as if he's playing a harsh game.
It's been almost a week and he's nowhere in sight.
I'm trying to figure out if this relationship is worth the fight.
When we first met, we've clicked from the start.
Some how I just knew that he would touch my heart.
I knew there would be issues but none quite like this.
He has a baby momma who gets me quite sick.
He lets her control every single thing we do.
I tried to tell him, honey she's in love with you.
I know the logical thing to do is leave him alone and find someone else.
I can't ladies and gentlemen I'm too much in love with and, there isn't anybody else.

I think…

These Four Words

These four words I love to say.
I know it's true every time I pray.
I say these words to make it through.
If you hear these words it will up lift you.
To bring you out of the darkness and into the light.
To help you say a prayer during the day and before you go to bed at night.
If you say these four words and truly believe.
Through Christ you'll see all you may achieve.
Let's come together and say these words.
Let's shout it from the roof tops and all to the worlds.
Let's say Yes Jesus Loves Me.
Now I guess you're wondering how I know.
Besides all that he's done, the Bible tells us so.

This Can Be You

Feelings of anger,
Feelings of pain.
Seeking a stranger,
Walking aimlessly in the rain.
Wondering where you possibly went wrong.
A person shot you down pretty strong.

Knowing your rights.
Knowing your ways.
Staying away from fights.
Staying away from strays.

Picking up a bottle.
Putting it to your lips.
Missing your person dottle,
Working to make tips.

You're not an even a bum.
You may be a woman or a man.
This stranger can really turn out to become
You if they really can.

To handsome 2000 from shygurl 2.5

Where an I going? Why am I here?
I want you to love me, yet I won't let you near.
I want to look into your eyes and yet I'm quite shy.
When you're not looking I see you and want to say.
I can't wait to go to sleep and wake to see you the very next day.
What am I going to do? How much more can I take?
I guess I better step up before you end up with a girl that's so fake.
I'm going to open up now and tell this to you.
I really, really like you and I don't know now what else I'm going to do!

Unacceptance of My Brother's Death

Losing my brother, losing a friend.
Could this be the beginning or truly the end?
I can't believe he's gone; it's truly a shock.
When it finally settled in, it hit me like a rock.
He was so funny and so full of life.
He was so close to having what he truly wanted, which was a loving wife.
I feel so blessed for having crossed his path.
His death is so hard to understand, just like some difficult math.
I really can't accept it, this really isn't true.
I feel as if I'll wake up and he'll say "girl, what's the matter with you?"
Then we'll all laugh and laugh all through the night.
Then I'll crack a joke and he'll say "You ain't right!"

We love you Aaron. May God bless and keep you always!
He died March 16th, 2005

Unfaithful Friend

I want you to do me a favor and open your eyes.
You birth many kids in this world, you don't have any, aren't you surprised.
There's a man in your life who taught you to use me.
I took over your life and made you believe that the way your life turned out is the way it has to be.
Look at you now. I made you fall.
You used to be so pretty and without me you could've had it all.
A good man, because you would've had the sense to let the bad one go.
All of your children especially your younger ones you didn't get to know.
I took away you intelligence and yet you haven't stopped.
When was the last time I allowed you to take a bath or even to mop?
I took you from your first child, in which you knew first.
This is all so funny to me; I'm with laughter going to burst.
Now because I told you to, you may now close your eyes.
I will continue to fill your system with filth and your head with believable lies.
However, as long as I continue to multiply and there's more people like you.
I'll never go a way and they'll be more who'll want me and will do what they have to do.
I bet all of you people out there are wondering who I am. All you have to do is look under some user's rugs.
By the way it's me, my name…DRUGS.

You Really Don't Know Me
So STOP TALKING

People say they know me but they never really get the chance to really look inside.
You look at me and assume this and then you assume that like I'm full of foolish pride.
Do you know what I see when I look at a tree?
Do you know what I think when I see a busy bumble bee?
Do you understand how I truly feel?
Do you know what's on my mind when I get down on my knees to kneel?
I have news for you, you do not.
You assume every time I go out with someone of the opposite sex that I'm hot.
You assume because I don't like to dress up, I'm some sort of dyke.
However if you get to know me, you'll see exactly what I'm like.
Do you understand the beauty that I see when I look at the purple color of the skies?
Do you understand the beauty I see in my mother's color changing eyes?
Do you understand how I feel when I see someone in pain?
Can't you feel the romance I feel when I'm staring at the pouring down rain?
Do you know why I look up to the sky at night and look at the twinkling stars?
Do you understand the need to escape when I used to hang out at the bars?
Do you understand why I have the starving need to feel loved?
Do you understand how much I used to get shoved?

You never take the chance to really get to know me.
You'll never get to see all I can be.
Yet you steady trying to judge me and all the nasty things you're going to say.
Unfortunately for you, you've lost a possible best friend today.

You Stupid, Stupid Fool

You fool, oh you fool.
You stupid, stupid fool.
Do you really think the way you act is really cool?
It's time for me to take your sorry ass to school.
To reach you the human code rule.

You can never understand
Your foolish ways seems to be on high demand.
You go to church here, you go to church there.
You keep a liquor bottle here; you keep a liquor bottle near.
Then you go to church grinning from ear to ear.
When deep down inside you don't even fear.
The fact God is still seeing.
All that we go and all we're believing.

You fool, you cosmic fool.
Do you really think doing drugs is cool?
Getting high in a car, getting high in the street.
Walking aimlessly at night, getting dirt on your feet.
You stupid, stupid fool
I think smacking you around is really cool.
I have a message for you.
The devil is waiting to do.
All the evil by letting you suffer and be in eternal pain.
You're going to miss being outside in the snow and sheltering
yourself from the pouring rain.
So you enjoy being a fool.
Being with the devil, man, isn't cool.

Author's Copy.

Thank you for all of your time and I hope that you had a good time reading my work. At times I had a great time writing and other times I didn't. I would like to thank you all for buying my book and I hope that you will continue to buy more of my work. My next book won't be poetry; it will be a story. I hope that you will love it and will recommend this and others to your friends.
Thank you and may GOD Bless and keep you always.

Kashavera Williams

P.S.

If you would like to e-mail me, you may do so at
kashaverawilliams@msn.com.
I hope to hear from you soon.